CONTENTS

D0257385

INTRODUCTION

Dear You

Welcome to your **Comic Relief Bake Off** booklet. By purchasing it you have already donated **£2 to Comic Relief**. For that we thank you and award you our star buyer badge.

You'll find your booklet as jam-packed as a Victoria Sponge with tasty tips, recipes and ideas to help you serve up delightful treats at a showstopping bake sale to raise money for **Red Nose Day 2015**.

But don't worry, there's not a technical challenge in sight. All the delicious bakes have been taken from Bake Off books and the recipes are so simple that even we could master them.

While your magnificent bakes are in the oven, turn over the page to read about how the dough you raise will go to help people living unimaginably tough lives both here in the UK and across Africa.

On your marks, get set, bake a fortune for Red Nose Day.

Mel and Sue

> **P.S.** If you want an extra serving of fundraising ideas, recipes and handy tools, download our free Great Comic Relief Bake Off Kit at rednoseday.com/bakeoffkit

HOW TO HOLD A SHOWSTOPPING BAKE SALE

Follow these tricks of the trade to make organising your bake sale as easy as pie. Don't worry, there's nothing technically challenging about any of them.

1 Ask friends, colleagues and family to join you. They could bake a few treats or help out on the day.

2 Pick a venue that you can use for free – your home, work, local sports centre, place of worship or community hall.

3 Once you've got a venue, make sure you set the date to avoid double bookings.

4 Time your bake sale for when people will want a nibble – during break times, lunch or afternoon tea.

5 Tell everyone about your bake sale in advance! Have a look at rednoseday.com/tools.

6 Make sure you've got sandwich bags or containers so everyone can take their cakes away.

7 Raise a little extra by selling tea and coffee with your cakes and soft drinks for the little ones.

8 Have a list of ingredients for people with allergies and label your nut-free or gluten-free bakes.

9 Bring enough spare change and make your cake prices round numbers to make things easier.

THE REAL iCiNG ON THE CAKE

Not only will you get to treat your friends, family or colleagues to some delicious bakes, the money you raise will go to helping people living incredibly difficult lives in the UK and across Africa.

Thank you.

 £40 could provide four young carers in the UK with a fun activity day, giving them a much-needed break from their huge responsibilities at home

 £65 could buy a bicycle for a health worker in Tanzania so they can give vital health advice to pregnant women living in remote villages

 £180 is enough to pay for three orphaned children in Zambia to go to school for a year

Chewy apricot cookies

Very quick to put together and bake, these almondy cookies – rather like a British version of soft amaretti – are sandwiched with butter icing or apricot conserve. The icing can be used plain or flavoured (see step 4), and can be tinted by adding edible food colouring, a couple of drops at a time. The quantities here make more than enough to sandwich the cookies, or to decorate 24 fairy cakes, or to fill and top a 20cm sponge.

MAKES 8 SANDWICH COOKIES

125g self-raising flour

50g ground almonds

100g caster sugar

100g unsalted butter, chilled and diced

1 medium free-range egg

3–4 drops almond extract

20g flaked almonds

200g apricot conserve (optional)

icing sugar, for dusting

FOR THE BUTTER ICING

125g unsalted butter, softened

400g icing sugar

3–4 tablespoons milk

1 teaspoon vanilla extract

1 Heat the oven to 160°C/325°F/gas 3. Line 1 or 2 baking sheets with baking parchment.

2 Sift the flour, ground almonds and caster sugar into a mixing bowl. Add the butter and rub in with your fingertips until the mixture looks like coarse crumbs. Beat the egg with the almond extract in a small bowl using a fork, just to mix, then add to the flour mixture. Beat with a wooden spoon for a few seconds so it is thoroughly combined.

3 Tip the dough onto a work surface. Lightly dust your hands with flour, then roll the mixture into 16 walnut-sized balls. Arrange them on the prepared baking sheets, spaced well apart to allow for spreading (it might be necessary to bake in batches). Scatter the flaked almonds on top of the balls and press in very gently. Bake for 14–17 minutes, until golden and just firm when gently pressed.

4 Meanwhile, make the icing. Put the butter into a bowl and beat by hand or machine until pale and creamy. Sift in the icing sugar, add the milk and vanilla, and beat (slowly if using a machine) until very smooth and thick. The icing can be used just as it is, but to make chocolate flavour, replace the vanilla with 3 tablespoons of cocoa powder. To make coffee butter icing, replace the milk with cold, very strong black coffee.

5 Remove the cookies from the oven and leave to cool on the baking sheets before peeling off the parchment. Use the butter icing or apricot conserve to sandwich pairs of cookies together, flat side in, then dust with icing sugar. Store in an airtight container and eat within 5 days.

Vanilla cupcakes

Homemade cakes always taste the best, even if you are only using them for some very creative decorating. Why not try all three flavours of icing?

MAKES 12

175g unsalted butter, at room temperature

3 eggs, at room temperature

100ml milk, at room temperature

250g caster sugar

250g self-raising flour

1 teaspoon vanilla extract

coloured sprinkles, honeycomb, and raspberries to decorate

FOR THE VANILLA/ RASBERRY ICING

75g unsalted butter, at room temperature

250g icing sugar

1 teaspoon vanilla extract

4 tablespoons milk or 60g raspberries

FOR THE CHOCOLATE FUDGE ICING

100g dark chocolate, broken into pieces

1 tablespoon golden syrup

25g unsalted butter

1 Heat the oven to 180°C/350°F/gas 4. Line a 12-hole bun tray with paper cases.

2 Put the butter, eggs and milk into a large bowl. Add the sugar, flour and vanilla extract and beat well, scraping down the sides of the bowl from time to time, until the mixture is smooth, creamy and fluffy.

3 Spoon the mixture into the paper cases, making sure they are evenly filled. Bake for 25–30 minutes, until well risen and golden brown, and a skewer or cocktail stick inserted in a central cake comes out clean. If not, bake for 2 more minutes, then test again.

4 Set the tray aside to cool for 2 minutes, then transfer the cupcakes to a wire rack and leave until completely cold.

5 To make vanilla icing, put the butter, icing sugar, vanilla extract and milk into a small bowl and beat well for about 3 minutes, until light and creamy.

6 For raspberry icing, make the vanilla icing above but replace the milk with raspberries and mix well so that the berries colour and flavour the icing evenly.

7 For the chocolate fudge topping, add the dark chocolate, golden syrup and butter to a small heatproof bowl. Bring a pan a third full of water to the boil, then turn off the heat and set the bowl over the pan. Stir gently with a wooden spoon until the icing is smooth and melted. Leave to cool for about 5 minutes until the mixture is thick enough to spread.

8 Using a round-bladed knife, spread or swirl the icing onto the cold cupcakes, then scatter the sprinkles, honeycomb or raspberries on top. Store in an airtight container and eat within 4 days.

Choc chip sandwiches

You can sandwich these using the butter icing on page 6, or for the ultimate treat, sandwich two of these chocolatey cookies together with a scoop of ice cream.

MAKES 24

125g unsalted butter, at room temperature

200g light brown muscovado sugar

1 medium free-range egg, lightly beaten

220g plain flour

3 tablespoons cocoa powder

¾ teaspoon baking powder

200g extras, e.g. white, milk or dark choc chips or chunks, OR walnut, pecan or brazil nut pieces

1 Heat the oven to 180°C/350°F/gas 4. Line 2 or 3 baking sheets with baking parchment (if you have only 1 sheet, bake the cookies in batches).

2 Put the butter and sugar into a mixing bowl and beat by hand or machine until the mixture looks creamy, smooth and fluffy. Using a spatula, scrape down the sides of the bowl from time to time so that everything gets thoroughly beaten.

3 Add the egg and beat well. Sift the flour, cocoa and baking powder into the bowl and mix with a wooden spoon. When uniformly chocolate brown with no streaks, tip in your chosen extras and mix again until evenly distributed.

4 Dip your hands in cold water, shake off the drops, then shape the dough into pingpong-sized balls. (If the dough gets sticky, dip your hands in water again.) Arrange the balls on the prepared sheets, spacing them well apart.

5 Bake for 15 minutes, until slightly darker around the edges. Set aside to cool completely before removing the cookies from the sheets. Store in an airtight container and eat within 5 days.

Chocolate fudge brownies

Very dark, dense and intensely fudgy, these chocolate brownies are
made the easy way – all in one pan with just a wooden spoon. You can
add your own contrast of texture, such as nuts, dried fruit or more chocolate.
Very good with a scoop of vanilla ice cream.

MAKES 16

**100g pecan halves OR
soft-dried morello/
sour cherries OR white
chocolate chips**

175g unsalted butter

65g cocoa powder

340g caster sugar

**2 medium free-
range eggs, at room
temperature**

**1 teaspoon vanilla
extract**

100g plain flour

salt

1 Heat the oven to 180°C/350°F/gas 4. Grease a 20cm
square brownie or cake tin and line the bottom with baking
parchment.

2 If using pecans rather than cherries or chocolate chips, place
them in a small tin or baking dish and toast them in the oven
for 5 minutes (this will give them a deeper flavour). Set aside to
cool, then roughly chop.

3 Put the butter into a saucepan that is large enough to hold
all the ingredients. Set over a low heat and melt the butter
gently, stirring every now and then.

4 Transfer the pan to a heatproof surface and sift in the cocoa.
Stir with a wooden spoon until smooth, then mix in the sugar.

5 Beat the eggs and vanilla together using a fork until just
combined, then stir into the cocoa mixture. Sift the flour and
a couple of pinches of salt into the pan and stir well, until
you can no longer see any streaks of flour. Mix in the nuts or
cherries or chocolate chips.

6 Transfer the mixture to the prepared tin and spread evenly.
Bake for about 30 minutes, until a wooden cocktail stick
inserted halfway between the side of the tin and the centre
of the cake comes out clean. The centre will still be a bit soft
or moist, but the mixture will continue cooking for a few
minutes after it comes out of the oven, and you don't want the
brownies to be dry or cake-like.

7 Set the tin on a wire rack. Run a round-bladed knife around
the inside of the tin to loosen the brownie cake, then leave
to cool. When cold, cut into 16 squares. Store in an airtight
container for up to 5 days.

Teatime biscuits

These are really fun, and you can be as creative as you like, trying different shapes and adding as little or as much decoration as you fancy – the photograph shows the biscuits topped with royal icing but you can try anything! Ideally, make the biscuits the day before icing them, and leave plenty of time for the icing to dry.

MAKES 18

115g unsalted butter, softened

100g caster sugar

finely grated zest of ½ unwaxed orange

1 large free-range egg yolk, at room temperature

85g ground almonds

225g plain flour

good pinch of salt

¼ teaspoon baking powder

½ teaspoon ground cinnamon

1 tablespoon orange juice

beaten egg, to glaze (optional)

1 Put the butter, sugar and orange zest in a large bowl and beat by hand or machine until creamy. Beat in the egg yolk followed by the almonds. Sift in the flour, salt, baking powder and cinnamon, then add the orange juice. Work the ingredients together, first with a wooden spoon, then with your hands, to make a fairly firm dough. Alternatively, process the mixture until the dough just comes together.

2 Wrap the dough in clingfilm and chill for about 15 minutes, until firm enough to roll out. (If tightly wrapped, the dough can be kept in the fridge for up to 5 days; if it gets very hard, leave at room temperature for 30 minutes or so before rolling out.)

3 Roll out the dough on a lightly floured work surface to the thickness of a £1 coin. Using 7–8cm shaped biscuit cutters dipped in flour, stamp out shapes from the dough. Arrange them, spaced slightly apart, on 2 baking sheets lined with baking parchment and chill for 15 minutes. Meanwhile, heat the oven to 180°C/350°F/gas 4.

4 If you aren't going to ice the biscuits, brush them with beaten egg. Bake for 10–12 minutes, until lightly golden, rotating the sheets if necessary so that they cook evenly. Allow to cool and firm up on the sheets for 5 minutes before carefully transferring the biscuits to a wire rack. When cold, you can ice and decorate them. Store in an airtight container and eat within a week.

Oat and raisin biscuits

These simple biscuits are always popular, and really easy for kids to make. For the best results use regular porridge oats rather than instant oats or porridge mix. Jumbo oats will give the biscuits a slightly chewy texture and lacy appearance. For a change, you could replace the vanilla with several gratings of nutmeg.

MAKES 30

125g unsalted butter, softened

150g light brown muscovado sugar

1 large free-range egg, at room temperature

1 tablespoon full-fat OR semi-skimmed milk

½ teaspoon vanilla extract

100g self-raising flour

75g raisins

150g porridge oats

1 Heat the oven to 180°C/350°F/gas 4. Grease 1 or 2 baking sheets.

2 Put the butter and sugar into a bowl and beat by hand or machine until pale and fluffy.

3 Put the egg, milk and vanilla in a separate bowl and beat until just combined. Pour into the butter mixture and beat well. Add the flour, raisins and oats and mix thoroughly with a wooden spoon.

4 Put heaped teaspoonfuls of the mixture on the prepared baking sheets, spacing them well apart to allow for spreading. (Bake in batches if necessary.) Bake for 12–15 minutes, or until the biscuits are lightly browned around the edges.

5 Set aside to firm up on the sheets for a few minutes, then transfer to a wire rack and leave until completely cold. Store the biscuits in an airtight container and eat within 5 days.

Florentines

These rich little morsels of nuts, fruit and chocolate make a delicious teatime treat, but are also a sophisticated alternative to after-dinner mints.

MAKES 18

50g unsalted butter

50g demerara sugar

50g golden syrup

50g plain flour

25g dried cranberries, finely chopped

50g candied peel, finely chopped

25g blanched almonds, finely chopped

25g walnut pieces, finely chopped

200g dark chocolate (70% cocoa solids)

1 Heat the oven to 180°C/350°F/gas 4. Line 3 baking sheets with baking parchment.

2 Measure the butter, sugar and syrup into a saucepan and heat gently until the butter has melted.

3 Remove the pan from the heat and stir in the flour, cranberries, candied peel and nuts.

4 Place 6 separate teaspoonfuls of the mixture on each baking sheet, spacing them well apart to allow plenty of room for spreading.

5 Bake for 8–10 minutes, until golden brown. Set aside on the sheets to cool and firm up, then use a palette knife to transfer the florentines to a wire rack. If they have become too hard to remove, pop them back into the oven for a few moments to soften.

6 Break 100g of the chocolate into a heatproof bowl set over a pan of simmering water. Stir frequently until the chocolate melts. Meanwhile, finely chop the remaining chocolate.

7 Carefully remove the bowl from the pan, add the chopped chocolate and stir gently until smooth. Keep stirring until the chocolate has cooled slightly.

8 Spread a little melted chocolate over the flat base of each florentine. Cool slightly before marking a zigzag pattern with a fork. Leave to set, chocolate side up, on the wire rack or baking parchment. Store in an airtight container.

Sticky maple-apple traybake

Here, tart-sweet Bramley apples are baked into a very light sponge that is bursting with flavour and finished with an easy-to-make creamy maple topping.

MAKES 20 PIECES

400g Bramley apples

¾ teaspoon ground cinnamon

2 teaspoons maple syrup

125ml sunflower oil

150g light brown muscovado sugar

½ teaspoon vanilla extract

grated zest of ½ unwaxed lemon

2 large free-range eggs

50g walnut pieces

275g plain flour

½ teaspoon baking powder

1 teaspoon bicarbonate of soda

good pinch of salt

2 large free-range egg whites, at room temperature

FOR THE TOPPING

75g unsalted butter, softened

75g light brown muscovado sugar

3 tablespoons maple syrup

175g full-fat cream cheese

1 Heat the oven to 180°C/350°F/gas 4. Grease a shallow 25 x 20cm baking tin and line the bottom with baking parchment.

2 Peel and core the apples, then cut into 1cm chunks. Put into a bowl, sprinkle with the cinnamon and toss until combined. Drizzle over the maple syrup and set aside.

3 Put the oil, sugar, vanilla and lemon zest into a bowl and whisk thoroughly. Lightly beat the eggs with a fork to break them up, then add to the bowl and whisk for a couple of minutes, until the mixture looks thick and slightly mousse-like.

4 Stir in the nuts and apple mixture using a large metal spoon. Sift the flour, baking powder, bicarbonate of soda and salt into the bowl and fold together – the mixture will be quite stiff.

5 Put the egg whites into a separate bowl and whisk until stiff peaks form. Fold into the apple mixture in 3 batches. Transfer to the prepared tin and spread evenly.

6 Bake for 30–35 minutes, or until a good golden brown and a skewer inserted into the centre of the cake comes out clean. Transfer the tin to a wire rack. Run a round-bladed knife around the inside of the tin to loosen the sponge, then leave to cool before turning out.

7 To make the topping, beat the butter with the sugar and maple syrup until smooth and creamy. Beat in the cream cheese.

8 Spread the topping evenly over the cooled sponge. Set aside in a cool spot to firm up, then cut into pieces. Store in an airtight container in a cool place and eat within 4 days.

Ginger and treacle spiced traybake

Dark, moist and spicy, this bake is stuffed with tiny pieces of stem ginger. Treacle can be difficult to weigh accurately as it tends to stick, so place the mixing bowl on the scales and weigh all the ingredients directly into it.

MAKES 15–20 PIECES

225g baking margarine or unsalted butter, softened

175g light brown muscovado sugar

200g black treacle

300g self-raising flour

2 teaspoons baking powder

1 teaspoon ground mixed spice

1 teaspoon ground allspice

4 medium free-range eggs, at room temperature

4 tablespoons milk

3 pieces (about 60g) stem ginger in syrup, drained and finely chopped

FOR THE ICING

75g icing sugar

3 tablespoons ginger syrup from the jar

3 pieces (about 60g) stem ginger in syrup, drained and finely chopped

1 Heat the oven to 160°C/325°F/gas 3. Grease a shallow baking tin (about 30 x 23 x 4cm), then line with baking parchment.

2 Measure all the cake ingredients straight into a large bowl. Beat well by hand or machine for about 2 minutes, scraping down the sides from time to time to make sure everything is thoroughly combined.

3 Using a spatula, scrape the mixture into the prepared tin and gently level the surface. Bake for 35–40 minutes, until the centre of the sponge springs back when pressed lightly with a finger, and the edges are beginning to shrink away from the sides of the tin.

4 Allow to cool for a few minutes, then ease the paper away from the sides of the tin and turn the sponge onto a wire rack. Peel off the paper, turn the sponge right way up and leave to cool completely.

5 To make the icing, sift the sugar into a bowl, add the ginger syrup and stir together until smooth. Pour the icing over the cold cake and spread out gently to the edges using a small palette knife. Sprinkle the chopped ginger over the surface, then leave to set. Cut into squares or slices before serving.

Chocolate coffee fudge cake bites

All the chopping and mixing here is done quickly and effortlessly in a food processor. You just need to have everything weighed and ready before you start – the tin prepared, flour sifted, eggs beaten and coffee made. During baking the mixture turns into a very moist, brownie-like sponge that is not too sweet. The topping is simple too – just melt and mix.

MAKES 20 BITES

100g pecan halves

100g plain flour

1 teaspoon baking powder

½ teaspoon bicarbonate of soda

75g dark chocolate (70% cocoa solids), broken up

2 tablespoons cocoa powder

200g light brown muscovado sugar

100ml hot black coffee (instant or made in a cafetière)

2 large free-range eggs, at room temperature, beaten

175g unsalted butter, softened and cut into pieces

125ml soured cream

FOR THE ICING

75g dark chocolate (70% cocoa solids), broken up

25g unsalted butter

3 tablespoons icing sugar

2 tablespoons black coffee

1 Heat the oven to 160°C/325°F/gas 3. Grease a shallow 25 x 20cm baking tin and line the bottom with greased baking parchment.

2 Arrange the pecans in the prepared tin, pressing them onto the greased parchment.

3 Sift the flour, baking powder and bicarbonate of soda into a bowl, then set aside.

4 Put the chocolate, cocoa powder and 100g of the sugar into a food processor and process until the mixture looks sandy. With the machine running, pour the hot coffee through the feed tube and process until the chocolate has melted. Stop the machine and scrape down the sides of the bowl.

5 Add the eggs and the remaining sugar and process for 30 seconds. Scrape down the bowl again, then add the butter and run the machine for a minute. Scrape down the bowl once more, then add the soured cream and the flour mixture. Process until it becomes a smooth, streak-free batter.

6 Spoon the mixture over the nuts in the baking tin. Bake for about 45 minutes, or until the sponge has started to shrink away from the sides of the tin and a skewer inserted into the centre comes out clean. The top crust will be only just firm.

7 Run a round-bladed knife around the inside of the tin to loosen the sponge , then set aside to cool in the tin. When cold, place a board over the tin and invert both. Lift off the tin and the lining paper – the nutty base is now the top.

8 To make the icing, put the chocolate into a small, heavy-based pan with the butter, icing sugar and coffee. Place over the lowest possible heat and stir gently until melted and smooth. Set aside until thick enough to spread. Cover the top of the cake with the icing and leave to set before cutting. Store in an airtight container and eat within 4 days.

Orange and olive oil loaf

Made with white spelt flour, which has a nuttier taste than regular plain flour, this unusual cake is quick to put together. Olive oil adds a gentle fruity flavour and moist texture. There's no need to use an expensive oil – for the best results pick one that's fairly light and just mildly peppery.

MAKES A 900G LOAF CAKE

2 medium free-range eggs, at room temperature

125ml mild fruity extra virgin olive oil

finely grated zest of 1 large unwaxed orange

175ml semi-skimmed OR full-fat milk

200g caster sugar

200g white spelt flour, or plain flour

½ teaspoon baking powder

½ teaspoon bicarbonate of soda

good pinch of salt

1 tablespoon warmed marmalade, to finish

1 Heat the oven to 160°C/325°F/gas 3. Grease a 900g loaf tin (about 26 x 13 x 8cm) and line with a long strip of baking parchment to cover the bottom and 2 short sides.

2 Break the eggs into a large bowl. Add the oil, orange zest and milk and mix with a balloon whisk until thoroughly combined. Whisk in the sugar.

3 Sift the flour, baking powder, bicarbonate of soda and salt into the bowl and mix well with a wooden spoon to make a smooth but runny batter.

4 Pour the mixture into the prepared tin and spread evenly. Bake for 55–60 minutes, until risen and golden brown, and a skewer inserted into the centre comes out clean.

5 Place the tin on a wire rack and immediately brush the top of the loaf with the warm marmalade. Run a round-bladed knife around the cake to loosen it, then leave to cool completely before removing it from the tin. Store in an airtight container and eat within 5 days.

Blueberry Bakewell tarts

Like the large version of Bakewell tart, these small ones have a frangipane filling, but include an unusual jam that is really simple and quick to make. If you're short of time, use 2 tablespoons shop-bought wild blueberry conserve or jam instead.

MAKES 12

55g unsalted butter, softened

55g caster sugar

1 large egg, beaten

40g ground almonds

15g plain flour

FOR THE BLUEBERRY JAM

125g blueberries, fresh or frozen

1 tablespoon caster sugar

squeeze of lemon juice

FOR THE PASTRY

200g plain flour

100g unsalted butter, chilled and cubed

40g icing sugar, sifted

1 large egg, beaten

TO DECORATE

50g icing sugar, sifted

fresh blueberries

1 First make the jam. Combine all the ingredients for it in a small saucepan and heat gently until the berries start to burst. Cook for a few minutes, until the mixture is very thick and has lost its watery appearance. Press through a sieve to remove the fruit skins, then allow to cool completely.

2 To make the pastry, sift the flour in a bowl and rub in the butter until the mixture resembles fine breadcrumbs. Stir in the sugar. Using a palette knife, cut in the beaten egg, then press together to form a ball of dough. Wrap in clingfilm and chill for at least 30 minutes.

3 Grease a 12-hole, preferably non-stick muffin tray. Roll out the pastry between a sheet of greaseproof paper and the clingfilm to a thickness of 3mm. Using a 5cm round cutter, stamp out 12 circles and use them to line the bottom of each hole in the prepared tray. Reroll the pastry and cut 12 strips 20cm long and 1cm wide. Use these to line the sides of each hole, pressing carefully to seal the seam and making sure there are no gaps. Chill for 15 minutes.

4 Heat the oven to 160°C/325°F/gas 3. Meanwhile, make the frangipane. Place the butter, sugar, egg, ground almonds and flour in a bowl and beat with an electric mixer until smooth and thoroughly combined.

5 Carefully prick the bottom of each pastry case with a fork. Place ½ teaspoon of the jam in each one. Top with the almond mixture, then bake for about 25 minutes, until the filling is risen and golden. Cool in the tray for a few minutes, then transfer to a wire rack to cool completely.

6 Mix the icing sugar with a little water to form a runny paste, then spoon into an icing bag. Use to decorate the cooled tarts, then top each with 1 or 2 fresh blueberries.

THANK YOU

Huge thanks to everyone who helped put this book together
Cristian Barnett, Dan Jones, Kristin Perers, Maja Smend, Chris Terry,
Mark Bourdillion, Anna Beattie, Rupert Frisby, Hannah Griffiths,
Kevin Cahill, Anne-Cecile Berthier, Kate De Quidt, Lucille Flood, Emily James,
Carole Winter, Rebecca Treadway, Chris Wilson, Nicky Ross, Sarah Hammond,
Claudette Morris, Bobby Birchall, the BBC Books team at Ebury Publishing,
Penguin Random House UK.

First published in Great Britain in 2015
by Hodder & Stoughton
An Hachette UK company

1

Recipes by Linda Collister © Love Productions
Photography by Cristian Barnett, Dan Jones and
Kristin Perers © Woodlands Books Ltd and
Maja Smend and Chris Terry
Photography on page 3 © Love Productions 2014
Other photography by Tom Dymond,
Annelaure Pothin, Jonathan Banks, Lucille Flood
Design by Bobby Birchall, Bobby&Co

All the recipes from this booklet were taken
from *The Great British Bake Off: How to Bake,
The Great British Bake Off: How to Turn Everyday
Bakes into Showstoppers, The Great British Bake Off:
Learn to Bake, The Great British Bake Off: Everyday*
and *The Great British Bake Off: Big Book of Baking.*

A CIP catalogue record for this title is available
from the British Library

ISBN 978 1 473 61666 0

Printed and bound in Germany
by GGP Media GmbH, Pößneck

Hodder & Stoughton Ltd
338 Euston Road
London NW1 3BH

www.hodder.co.uk

**Comic Relief, registered charity
326568 (England Wales); SCO39730
(Scotland)**